2. *Gloria*

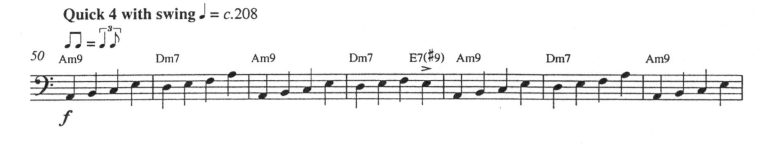

T0056050

3. *Sanctus*

Straight quavers; bass plays roots throughout.

4. *Benedictus*

Straight quavers

5. *Agnus Dei*

Straight quavers; bass plays almost exclusively roots.

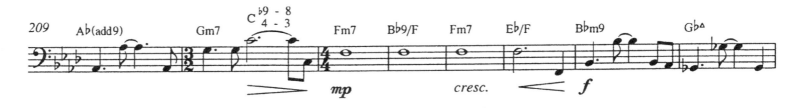

ISBN 978-0-19-335655-9

A Little Jazz Mass

Bob Chilcott

for choir, piano, and optional bass and drum kit

This bass part may be played as written or used as a guide from which the player may improvise freely.

A Little Jazz Mass is available in versions for upper voices (SSA) and mixed voices.

This bass part was prepared by Alexander Hawkins.

Duration: *c.*12 minutes

Double Bass

A Little Jazz Mass

1. *Kyrie*

Bob Chilcott

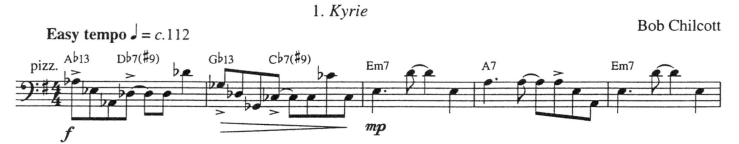

Straight quavers; bass plays almost exclusively roots, 5ths, and 7ths.

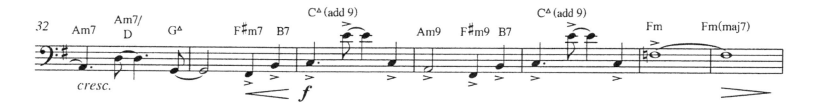

poco rit.

© Oxford University Press 2004 and 2006
Bob Chilcott has asserted his right under the Copyright, Designs and Patents Act, 1988, to be identified as Composer of this Work.

OXFORD UNIVERSITY PRESS, MUSIC DEPARTMENT, GREAT CLARENDON STREET, OXFORD OX2 6DP
Photocopying this copyright material is ILLEGAL.

ISBN 978-0-19-335655-9

9 780193 356559